# Lowriders

## J. Poolos

TRADUCCIÓN AL ESPAÑOL:
Eduardo Alamán

**PowerKiDS** press. & **Editorial Buenas Letras**™
New York

Published in 2008 by The Rosen Publishing Group, Inc.
29 East 21st Street, New York, NY 10010

Copyright © 2008 by The Rosen Publishing Group, Inc.

First Edition

Editor: Amelie von Zumbusch
Book Design: Greg Tucker and Lissette González
Photo Researcher: Nicole Pristash

Photo Credits: Cover © Robert Yager/Getty Images; pp. 5, 11, 13, 19 © Ron Kimball/Ron Kimball Stock; pp. 7, 9 © Shutterstock.com; p. 15 © Frank Micelotta/Getty Images; p. 17 © Sandy Huffaker/Getty Images; p. 21 © Matthew Peyton/Getty Images.

Cataloging Data

Poolos, Jamie.
    Lowriders / J. Poolos; traducción al español: Eduardo Alamán. — 1st ed.
        p. cm. — (Wild rides—Autos de locura)
    Includes index.
    ISBN-13: 978-1-4042-7636-9 (library binding)
    ISBN-10: 1-4042-7636-X (library binding)
    1. Lowriders—Juvenile literature. 2. Spanish language materials  I. Title.

Manufactured in the United States of America

## Web Sites

Due to the changing nature of Internet links, PowerKids Press and Editorial Buenas Letras have developed an online list of Web sites related to the subject of this book. This site is updated regularly. Please use this link to access the list: www.powerkidslinks.com/wild/low/

# Contents

# Contenido

A lowrider is a car or truck that has been changed so that it rides very low to the ground. Lowriders have flashy paint jobs, with **sparkles**, patterns, or pictures. They also have small **chrome** wheels that have **spokes**.

The insides of the cars are also fancy. The seats and doors are often covered with leather or a soft cloth called velvet.

---

Un lowrider es un auto o camión que ha sido modificado para pasear muy cerca del suelo. Los lowriders están pintados con **destellos** o diseños muy llamativos. También tienen llantas con rines de **cromo** y **rayos**.

Por dentro, los lowriders también son muy atractivos. Con frecuencia, los asientos y las puertas están cubiertos de cuero o terciopelo.

Some lowriders are painted with brightly colored flames.

Algunos lowriders están pintados con llamas de colores brillantes.

Lowrider drivers use **hydraulics** to change how high their cars are. Hydraulics are a system of narrow tubes that join the car to its wheels. Car **batteries** push oil through the tubes and make the car go up and down. The driver works **switches** that control the flow of oil to each wheel. The driver raises and lowers the car by turning the switches on and off.

---

Los pilotos de lowriders usan la **hidráulica** para cambiar la altura de sus autos. Un sistema hidráulico usa tubos conectados a las ruedas. Las **baterías** del coche empujan aceite por los tubos y hacen que el auto suba o baje. El piloto controla los **interruptores** que regulan el aceite que pasa a las ruedas. Al encender o apagar los interruptores, el piloto hace brincar el auto.

This driver is using the car's hydraulics to make it bounce.

Este piloto usa el sistema hidráulico de su auto para hacerlo saltar.

Lowriders are built for show. The cars have special paint jobs that make them sparkle. The kind of paint used is called flake. Flake is made by mixing tiny bits of metal into the paint. Lowrider paint jobs often have flames or thin stripes called pinstripes. Some lowriders even have pictures painted on them.

---

Los lowriders se construyen para ser exhibidos. Por eso están pintados de manera brillante. A este tipo de pintura se le llama *flake,* que en español quiere decir "chispa". Para hacer las chispas, se mezcla la pintura con pequeños trozos de metal. Con frecuencia, a los lowriders les pintan llamas o rayas muy delgadas. A algunos lowriders les pintan fotografías.

You can see the painted flames in this picture of a lowrider.

En esta fotografía de un lowrider se pueden ver las llamas en la pintura.

The insides of the best lowriders are as striking as the outsides. These cars are covered in leather, velvet, and other cloths inside. Some owners add pieces of wood to the **dashboards** and doors. Whether the inside of a lowrider is **customized** or not, the car usually has a special steering wheel.

Por dentro, los lowriders son tan espectaculares como por fuera. Por dentro, los lowriders están cubiertos de cuero, terciopelo y otras telas. Algunos lowriders tienen madera en el **tablero de instrumentos** y las puertas. Aunque el interior de un lowrider no esté **personalizado,** con frecuencia tiene un volante especial.

The inside of this lowrider is covered in red velvet.

El interior de este lowrider está cubierto de terciopelo rojo.

11

Almost any car can be made into a lowrider. The original lowriders were made from cars from the 1950s, like the Mercury and the Chevrolet Deluxe. Today, cars like Buicks and Cadillacs are popular choices, but the Chevy Impala is the favorite among lowrider builders. The Chevy Impala is a two-door car from the 1960s.

Casi cualquier auto puede convertirse en un lowrider. Los primeros lowriders se hicieron de autos de los años cincuenta, como el Mercury y el Chevrolet Deluxe. Hoy, autos como los Buicks y los Cadillacs son populares, pero el auto favorito de los lowriders es el Chevy Impala. El Chevy Impala es un auto de dos puertas de los años sesenta.

This light blue lowrider is a 1962 Chevy Impala.

Este lowrider celeste es un Chevy Impala de 1962.

Lowriders started out in **Chicano culture**. They later became part of hip-hop culture. When hip-hop culture became widely popular in the 1990s, more and more people became interested in lowriders. The builders and painters of the coolest lowriders are well known in lowrider culture.

Los lowriders comenzaron en la **cultura chicana.** Más tarde, se hicieron populares entre los seguidores de hip-hop. Cuando la música hip-hop aumentó su popularidad en los años noventa, más y más personas se interesaron en los lowriders. Los constructores y pintores de los lowriders más espectaculares son muy conocidos entre los aficionados.

Rappers Eminem,
50 Cent,
and Dr. Dre are riding
in this lowrider.

Los raperos Eminem,
50 Cent y Dr. Dre
pasean en
un lowrider.

One of the chief activities that lowrider clubs take part in is the car show. At car shows, lowrider builders and owners gather to show off their work. Fans come to the shows to look at the cars and to vote for their favorites. The owner of the car that is judged best in show takes home a trophy, or prize.

Los clubs de lowriders participan en exposiciones de autos. En estas exposiciones, los dueños y los constructores de lowriders presumen sus autos. Muchos aficionados van a estas exposiciones para ver los autos y votar por sus favoritos. Al dueño del auto ganador del mejor lowrider en exposición se le da un premio, o trofeo.

These fans are looking at a lowrider in a car show in California.

Aficionados mirando un lowrider en una exposición en California.

17

At car shows, owners also use hydraulics to lift and lower lowriders in two kinds of contests, or games people try to win. In hopping contests, each driver tries to bounce his or her car the highest. In dancing contests, drivers complete a list of moves. These moves include bouncing, turning, and lifting the corners of the car one at a time.

---

En las exposiciones de autos, los dueños de lowriders usan hidráulica para participar en dos tipos de competencias. En la competencia de salto, los pilotos tratan de hacer brincar el auto tan alto como sea posible. En la competencia de danza, el piloto realiza varios movimientos. Estos movimientos pueden ser: rebotar, dar vueltas y levantar, una a una, las esquinas del auto.

**Dancing is one of the most popular events at lowrider car shows.**

La competencia de danza es muy popular en las exposiciones de lowriders.

19

Not all lowriders are cars. There are also lowrider motorcycles and bicycles. Bicycles and motorcycles do not use hydraulics, but they are low to the ground, like lowrider cars. Lowrider motorcycles have chrome wheels and flake paint jobs. A lowrider bicycle is a customized bicycle with a long, low seat, called a banana seat.

No todos los lowriders son autos. También hay motocicletas y bicicletas lowrider. A diferencia de los autos lowrider, las motos y bicicletas no usan sistemas hidráulicos para pasear cerca del suelo. Las motos lowrider tienen ruedas de cromo y pintura brillante. Una bicicleta lowrider es una bicicleta personalizada con un largo asiento llamado asiento banana.

**This is a lowrider motorcycle.**

---

*Esta es una motocicleta lowrider.*

Lowriders are a blast to drive and show off. Their paint jobs and customized insides show us that a car can be a work of art. It takes great skill and imagination to build a cool lowrider. As long as people enjoy bright, shiny, hopping, and dancing cars, lowriders will live forever.

---

Es muy divertido manejar y presumir un lowrider. Sus diseños e interiores personalizados nos enseñan que un auto puede ser una obra de arte. Para construir un lowrider se necesita mucha habilidad e imaginación. Mientras la gente disfrute estos brillantes autos brincadores y danzantes, los lowriders vivirán por siempre.

# Glossary

**batteries** (BA-tuh-reez) Things in which power is stored.

**Chicano** (chi-KAH-noh) Having to do with Americans whose families came from Mexico.

**chrome** (KROHM) A shiny metal that is used on cars and motorcycles.

**culture** (KUL-chur) The beliefs, practices, and arts of a group of people.

**customized** (KUS-tuh-myzd) Made or changed to suit a certain person.

**dashboards** (DASH-bordz) Flat places under the big window in the front of a car.

**hydraulics** (hy-DRO-liks) A system of tubes that lift and lower the body of a car when oil is pushed through them.

**sparkles** (SPAHR-kulz) Things that shine in quick flashes.

**spokes** (SPOHKS) Rods that connect the middle of a wheel to the wheel's edge.

**switches** (SWICH-ez) Tools used to operate a machine or control the flow of energy.

# Glosario

**baterías** (las) Objetos que almacenan energía.

**cromo** (el) Un metal brillante que se utiliza en autos y motocicletas.

**cultura chicana** (la) La forma de pensar y actuar de un grupo particular de personas cuyas familias vienen de México.

**destellos** (los) Cosas que brillan de forma intermitente.

**hidráulica** (la) El sistema de tubos que hace subir o bajar el auto cuando se le inyecta aceite.

**interruptores** (los) Aparato que se usa para controlar el paso de energía.

**personalizado** Algo hecho o modificado de acuerdo al gusto personal.

**rayos** (los) Varas de metal que conectan el centro de una rueda con su borde.

**tablero de instrumentos** (el) Lugar plano al frente del auto bajo el parabrisas.

# Index

# Índice